IT'S ELECTRIC!

Using Electricity

Chris Oxlade

www.raintreepublishers.co.uk

Visit our website to find out more information about Raintree books.

To order:
☎ Phone 0845 6044371
📄 Fax +44 (0) 1865 312263
💻 Email myorders@raintreepublishers.co.uk

Customers from outside the UK please telephone +44 1865 312262

Raintree is an imprint of Capstone Global Library Limited, a company incorporated in England and Wales having its registered office at 7 Pilgrim Street, London, EC4V 6LB – Registered company number: 6695582

Edited by Daniel Nunn, Rebecca Rissman, and Catherine Veitch
Designed by Joanna Hinton-Malivoire
Picture research by Elizabeth Alexander
Production by Eirian Griffiths
Originated by Capstone Global Library Ltd
Printed and bound in China by Leo Paper Products Ltd

ISBN 978 1 406 23230 1 (hardback)
15 14 13 12
10 9 8 7 6 5 4 3 2

ISBN 978 1 406 23235 6 (paperback)
16 15 14 13 12
10 9 8 7 6 5 4 3 2 1

British Library Cataloguing in Publication Data
Oxlade, Chris.
Using electricity. -- (It's electric!)
537-dc22
A full catalogue record for this book is available from the British Library.

Acknowledgements
The author and publisher are grateful to the following for permission to reproduce photographs: Alamy pp. 26 (© PhotoAlto), 27 (© Realimage), 29 (© Justin Kase z13z); © Capstone Publishers p. 18 (Karon Dubke); iStockphoto pp. 12 (© Gene Chutka), 23 (© ricardoazoury), 24 (© Andrew Howe), 25 (© Torsten Stahlberg); Shutterstock pp. 4 (© Sherri R. Camp), 5 (© sevenke), 6 (© Roger De Marfa), 7 (© yampi), 8 (© Rafa Irusta), 9 (© Chungking), 10 (© prism68), 11 (© Adrian Britton), 13 (© Discpicture), 14 (© Erzetic), 15 left (© Sideways Design), 15 right (© Esbobeldijk), 16 (© J van der Wolf), 17 (© Songquan Deng), 19 (© Tatiana Popova), 20 (© Grandpa), 21 (© Karnizz), 22 (© Baloncici), 28 (© Katharina Wittfeld).

Cover photograph of a harbour laser light show in Hong Kong reproduced with permission of Shutterstock (© markrhiggins). Design background feature reproduced with permission of Shutterstock (© echo3005).

The publisher would like to thank Terence Alexander for his assistance in the preparation of this book.

Every effort has been made to contact copyright holders of material reproduced in this book. Any omissions will be rectified in subsequent printings if notice is given to the publisher.

Contents

Some words are shown in bold, **like this**.
You can find them in the glossary on page 30.

Using electricity

Take a look around the room you are in. How many things in the room work using electricity? Count the ones that use **batteries** as well as household electricity. Don't forget the lights!

How many electric machines can you see here?

Electricity lights our streets and buildings.

Every day of our lives we use many electric machines. We use them at home, at school, at work, and in factories. It would be impossible to live our lives without electricity.

Electricity and energy

The energy in electricity lights up this stadium.

Electricity makes things work. It makes the motors in a washing machine spin, it makes music players give out sound, and it makes televisions show pictures. Electricity is a type of **energy**.

Electricity is a really useful type of energy. This is because we can change it into light, movement, or heat. Light, movement, and heat are types of energy, too.

An electric cooker turns electricity into heat.

Making electricity

Wind turbines make electricity from the energy in wind.

wind turbine

Most electricity is made at electricity generating stations. Here, energy is turned into electricity. Electricity is also made at **wind farms**, at **solar power stations**, and at **hydroelectric power stations**.

Electricity travels along thick cables from electricity generating stations to towns and cities. The cables are called power lines.

pylon

Power lines are held up by tall towers called pylons.

Electricity supply

Most homes have electricity that comes from electricity generating stations. The electricity reaches homes along cables, often under the ground. Schools, offices, factories, and other buildings also get electricity in this way.

Electricity cables are hidden in walls and floors, safely out of the way.

cable

More cables carry the electricity to wall sockets in each room in a home. When you push a plug into a socket, electricity can flow. Cables also carry electricity to light switches and fittings.

These sockets have switches to turn the electricity on and off.

Electricity at home

Electricity powers games consoles and televisions.

Electricity works many appliances and gadgets in our homes. It powers televisions, computers, radios, music players, and DVD players. It also powers cleaning and cooking machines.

Electricity does different jobs in many appliances. In a washing machine, it works the motor that turns the drum. It works the heater that heats the water, and it works the pump that gets rid of dirty water.

A washing machine washes clothes using the energy in electricity.

Electric light

We use lights in underground places.

We can turn electric lights on and off with the flick of a switch. Lights let us work and play indoors when it's dark. They also light up our streets, paths, gardens, and stadiums.

Light bulbs turn electricity into light. The most common kinds of light bulbs we use in our homes are LED bulbs and compact fluorescent tubes. LED is short for **light-emitting diode**. These bulbs do not use a lot of energy, so they last a long time.

LED

compact flourescent tube

Light for signs

tot het rode licht gedoofd is
er kan nog een trein komen

Coloured lights tell drivers when to stop and go.

We use electric lights for giving people information as well as for lighting up rooms. For example, small coloured **LEDs** tell us when a machine is switched on, or has finished doing its job.

Electronic signs are made up of LEDs. They give us information at railway stations and on buses. Lighting up different bulbs makes letters, numbers, and patterns.

The advertising signs on this street are made up of LEDs.

Batteries

We use batteries to power toys, phones, and other gadgets, and even electric vehicles. The **batteries** push electricity around an electric circuit. An electric **circuit** is a loop that electricity can flow around.

Batteries must be used with the "+" and "-" signs the right way round.

After a while all of the electricity in a battery is used up. When standard batteries are empty they must be thrown away. **Rechargeable** batteries can be refilled with electricity.

Rechargeable batteries can be used over and over again.

Electric transport

This car has been plugged into an electricity supply to **recharge** its batteries.

Many sorts of transport use electricity. Electric cars have large **batteries**. The batteries work an electric motor that turns the car's wheels. Electric wheelchairs and mobility scooters also have batteries and motors.

Electric trains are moved by powerful electric motors. Some get electricity from a cable above the track. Trams and trolley buses also work using electricity from cables above the streets.

cables

Electric trams are fast and quiet.

Electricity in industry

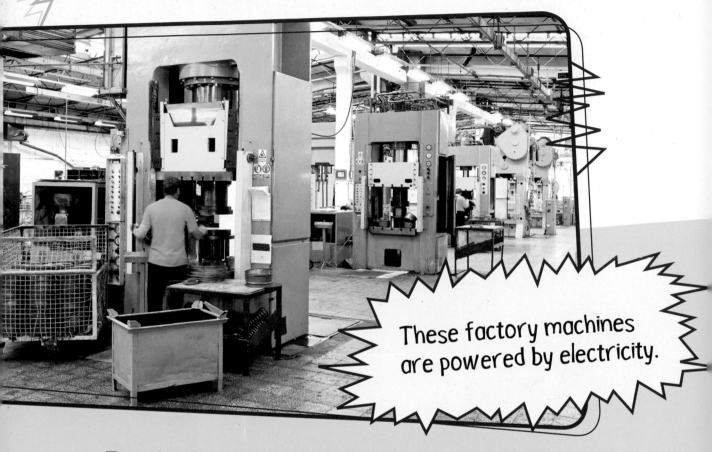

These factory machines are powered by electricity.

Factories need lots of electricity. Electric motors work machines that cut and shape materials such as metals and plastics. They also power machines such as conveyor belts that move materials.

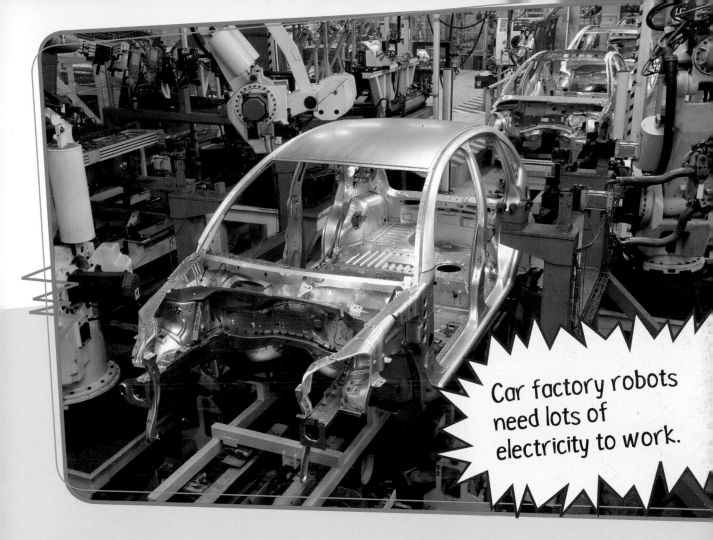

Car factory robots need lots of electricity to work.

In a car factory electricity works the tools that workers use to put cars together. Electricity also powers robots that glue the pieces of the cars' bodies together. Electricity lights and heats the factory, too.

Electronics

Machines and gadgets such as computers, calculators, cameras, and mobile telephones have very complicated electric **circuits**. The circuits are called electronic circuits.

There are hundreds of complicated electronic circuits inside a computer.

Electronics control what a machine does. For example, in a calculator the circuits do adding and subtracting, and show answers on a display.

A robot vacuum cleaner cleans a room on its own! It is controlled by electronics.

Saving electricity

Please turn off the lights

Switching off lights is an easy way to save electricity.

Most electricity is made by burning materials called **fossil fuels** in power stations. Burning fuels is not good for our environment. If we use less electricity we will do less damage. It also means we won't run out of fuel so quickly.

Modern electric machines are made so they use as little electricity as possible while they do their jobs. We say they are **energy-efficient** machines.

A label shows how good a machine is at saving energy.

Safe with electricity

Household electricity is very powerful. If it goes through a person, it can badly injure them. The electricity in power lines and in overhead cables on railways is even more dangerous. It can even kill a person.

Never ignore warning signs like this one.

Danger
High voltage

Never play with household electricity. Never push anything into an electricity socket or into a light fitting. Never take apart any electric machine or gadget. Then you won't get an electric shock.

This device has a special safety feature that switches off the electricity if there are problems.

Glossary

battery part that pushes electricity around a circuit

circuit loop that electricity flows around

energy something that can make things happen. Electricity, light, heat, and sound are all types of energy.

energy efficient machine that uses as little electricity as possible

fossil fuel material that is burnt to make heat, light, or power. Fossil fuels include wood, gas, oil, and coal.

hydroelectric power station place where electricity is made from the energy in flowing water

light-emitting diode (LED) small device that gives out light when electricity flows through it

rechargeable battery that can have electricity put back into it, so it can be used again

solar power station place where electricity is made from the energy in sunshine

wind farm place where electricity is made from the wind using wind turbines

Find out more

Books

Electricity Supply, James Nixon
(Franklin Watts, 2009)

The Facts about Electricity, Rebecca Hunter
(Franklin Watts, 2007)

Using Electricity (My World of Science),
Angela Royston (Raintree Publishers, 2008)

Websites

**powerup.ukpowernetworks.co.uk/under-11.
aspx**
Interactive stuff on electricity from this UK energy
distribution company.

**www.bbc.co.uk/schools/scienceclips/
ages/6_7/electricity.shtml**
Animated interactive games about electricity
from the BBC.

www.engineeringinteract.org/interact.htm
Fun electricity games from Cambridge University
(click on Silicon Spies).

Index